This Book Belongs To:

monthly prayers
for my
FUTURE HUSBAND

Becoming A Proverbs 31 Woman Before Marriage

PSALMFUL COLLECTION

PSALMFUL

Monthly Prayers for my Future Husband

Published by Psalmful LLC.
ISBN 9798-3613-222-68

Get in touch: info@psalmful.com
psalmful.com

DEDICATION

To every future wife waiting for her future husband, God hears your prayers and is pleased with your faith.

WHO CAN FIND A VIRTUOUS WOMAN? FOR HER PRICE IS FAR ABOVE RUBIES. THE HEART OF HER HUSBAND DOES SAFELY TRUST IN HER SO THAT HE SHALL HAVE NO NEED OF SPOIL. SHE WILL DO HIM GOOD AND NOT EVIL ALL THE DAYS OF HER LIFE. SHE SEEKS WOOL AND FLAX AND WORKS WILLINGLY WITH HER HANDS. SHE IS LIKE THE MERCHANTS' SHIPS; SHE BRINGS HER FOOD FROM AFAR. SHE RISES ALSO WHILE IT IS YET NIGHT AND GIVES MEAT TO HER HOUSEHOLD AND A PORTION TO HER MAIDENS. SHE CONSIDERS A FIELD AND BUYS IT: WITH THE FRUIT OF HER HANDS, SHE PLANTS A VINEYARD. SHE GIRDS HER LOINS WITH STRENGTH AND STRENGTHENS HER ARMS. SHE PERCEIVES THAT HER MERCHANDISE IS GOOD: HER CANDLE GOES NOT OUT BY NIGHT. SHE LAYS HER HANDS TO THE SPINDLE, AND HER HANDS HOLD THE DISTAFF. SHE STRETCHES OUT HER HAND TO THE POOR; YEA, SHE REACHES FORTH HER HANDS TO THE NEEDY. SHE IS NOT AFRAID OF THE SNOW FOR HER HOUSEHOLD: FOR ALL HER HOUSEHOLD ARE CLOTHED WITH SCARLET. SHE MAKES HERSELF COVERINGS OF TAPESTRY; HER CLOTHING IS SILK AND PURPLE. HER HUSBAND IS KNOWN IN THE GATES WHEN HE SITTETH AMONG THE ELDERS OF THE LAND. SHE MAKES FINE LINEN, SELLS IT, AND DELIVERS GIRDLES TO THE MERCHANT. STRENGTH AND HONOR ARE HER CLOTHING, AND SHE SHALL REJOICE IN TIME TO COME. SHE OPENS HER MOUTH WITH WISDOM, AND IN HER TONGUE IS THE LAW OF KINDNESS. SHE LOOKS WELL TO THE WAYS OF HER HOUSEHOLD AND EATS NOT THE BREAD OF IDLENESS. HER CHILDREN ARISE UP AND CALL HER BLESSED; HER HUSBAND ALSO, AND HE PRAISETH HER. MANY DAUGHTERS HAVE DONE VIRTUOUSLY, BUT YOU EXCEL THEM ALL. FAVOR IS DECEITFUL, AND BEAUTY IS VAIN: BUT A WOMAN THAT FEARS THE LORD, SHE SHALL BE PRAISED. GIVE HER OF THE FRUIT OF HER HANDS, AND LET HER OWN WORKS PRAISE HER IN THE GATES.

PROVERBS 31:10-31

CONTENTS

DECLARATION

But without faith it is impossible to please Him, for he who comes to God must believe that He is, and that He is a rewarder of those who diligently seek Him.

Hebrews 11:6

Dear Heavenly Father, I trust You with my life and my future. I trust that if I ask anything according to Your will, You hear me and will answer my prayers. I trust You will give me the grace I need to wait on You, Lord. I trust You will bless my future and will never leave or forsake me, in Jesus Name.

Use the blank lines to write the declaration statement and speak it over yourself.

_____

_____

_____

_____

_____

_____

_____

_____

_____

_____

_____

_____

_____

_____

_____

_____

MY CONTENTMENT

Trust in the Lord with all your heart, and lean not on your own understanding. In all your ways acknowledge Him, And He shall direct your paths.

Proverbs 3:5

DEAR HEAVENLY FATHER,

Thank You for giving me the desire for marriage and prolonging life on this earth by creating a family after your design. I pray You will provide contentment for me in the waiting season and prepare me to be a better wife. Help me strive to be myself first, what I pray for in my spouse. What awaits in the future, I can not know, but what I do know is what You've given me right now, and that is my body in this flesh to be a woman of God. Help me to love like You love, be found content in whatever comes my way, and surrender any feelings of lack or longing. I pray that, first and foremost, I will be satisfied in Your presence despite what I have or don't have. I thank You that You are working out everything for my good because I am called according to Your purpose. Help me to be satisfied in this season of being single and boldly say, "this is the day that the Lord has made. I will rejoice and be glad in it."

IN JESUS NAME I PRAY.

PRAYERS FOR HIM

Read these prayers for your future husband during the next thirty-one days, and use the blank lines to write down your personal prayers or thoughts. Repeat the prayers monthly.

RELATIONSHIP WITH GOD

And your ears shall hear a word behind you, saying, "This is the way, walk in it," when you turn to the right or when you turn to the left.

Isaiah 30:21

DEAR HEAVENLY FATHER,

Thank You for desiring to know and have fellowship with Your children. I pray for my future husband's relationship with You. Give him a longing to be with You and spend time with You. I pray he would be a man whose heart draws closer to You every day and would lead our home closer to You. I pray he would be passionate about serving You. I pray that You would call him Your friend. I pray his love for You would be visible in Word and action. I pray he wouldn't neglect spending time with You and would prioritize the secret place above everything. I pray he would have a love for Your Word and would meditate on it day and night. I pray we as a family would commit to drawing nearer to You every day and build our life from the quiet place. I pray that we would uplift one another and help keep each other going if one is down. I pray he would be more than a husband, but a spiritual partner who would pray for me and with me. Father, please encounter him, and may his faith grow strong as he comes up higher in Your presence. Give him assurance that You will fulfill the promises over his life as You promised. I pray his soul would long for You as a deer longs for streams of water and that he would seek Your face daily.

IN JESUS NAME I PRAY.

SALVATION

For by grace you have been saved through faith. And this is not your own doing, it is the gift of God.

Ephesians 2:8

DEAR HEAVENLY FATHER,

Thank You for Your Son, Jesus, and thank You for the gift of salvation. Thank You for Your kindness which leads to repentance, and thank You for being so good and forgiving. I pray for my future husband's walk with You. I pray that he will trust in Jesus and accept the free gift of eternal life. I pray he would endure till the very end, and after finishing the course, he would be found faithful and acceptable to You. I pray he will hear those beautiful words, "My good and faithful servant," after he finishes his course on earth. Father, I pray You would protect him from the advances of the enemy and keep him free from the entanglement of sin. Equip him for battle, to fight the good fight of faith, and I pray You would give him victory. May he be diligent and spend his time wisely here on earth. I pray he would store up for himself treasures in heaven and would live with an understanding that all of these worldly things will one day pass away. Help him to remain faithful to You all the days of his life, and I pray our union will be pleasing to You. Please sanctify our marriage on earth so that together, we will victoriously walk the finish line into heaven.

IN JESUS NAME I PRAY.

MAN OF PRAYER

I desire therefore that the men pray everywhere, lifting up holy hands without wrath and doubting.

1 Timothy 2:8

DEAR HEAVENLY FATHER,

I pray for my future husband's prayer life. Please bless him with a deep desire to spend time in Your presence. I pray he would pray everywhere and lift up his hands without wrath or doubt. I pray he would trust You as his provider and live in complete surrender to You. Father, I pray You would be the first place he goes when in trouble. I pray he would always rejoice, pray without ceasing, and in all circumstances give You thanks because this is Your will. Help him not to be anxious about anything, but in every situation to pray and petition with thanksgiving making his requests known to You. I pray he would have intimacy with You and hear Your voice. Remind him that You already know what he needs even before he asks. I pray he would enter Your throne room with boldness and find mercy and grace in time of need. May the beautiful character of Jesus be reflected in his life. May he have the ability to wait on You, Lord. I pray he would be a prayer warrior, interceding on behalf of our family together. Father, I pray our marriage will have a foundation of prayer. May our praying closets have a constant pleasant aroma going up to heaven, and I pray You, Lord, would be in the center of our lives.

IN JESUS NAME I PRAY.

LIFE OF SURRENDER

And we know that all things work together for good to those who love God, to those who are the called according to His purpose.
Romans 8:28

DEAR HEAVENLY FATHER,

Thank You for offering the ability to surrender everything to You. Thank You for willingly taking our loads and giving us peace. I pray for my future husband and ask that You would reveal to him the power of surrendering everything to You. Help him to let go of control and give him the faith to trust You completely. I ask that You would help him to surrender all of his burdens, worries, and fears to You. I pray that You would open the doors that need to be opened and close the doors that need to be closed for him. May his life be filled with miracles from You, Lord. I pray that he will surrender all past, present, and future issues to You. I pray he would have a humble heart that listens to wise advice, and may we always come before You with surrendered hearts in our marriage. I pray that You will help us to trust You with our hopes, plans, and dreams. May he not let things build up inside, but I pray he would quickly come before You in prayer. Please remind him that all things work together for good to those who love God and are called according to His purpose. Thank You that we don't have to be bound to fleshly ways but can surrender our will to Yours with the help of Your Holy Spirit.

IN JESUS NAME I PRAY.

INNER HEALING

Come to Me, all you who labor and are heavy laden, and I will give you rest. Take My yoke upon you and learn from Me, for I am gentle and lowly in heart, and you will find rest for your souls.

Matthew 11:28-29

Thank You for Your healing and peace. Thank You that because of Jesus, there is hope for the future and a light at the end of the tunnel. I pray for my future husband's inner state and that he would have Your peace dwelling inside his inner being. I pray for Your protection and healing from trauma, anxiety, and any pain of the past or present moment. I pray You would help him to forgive the things he remembers and mend any pain he may be carrying that causes him uneasiness and fill him with Your peace. I pray that You would give him the ability to always remain in prayer, forgiveness, and the power to reject lies and replace them with Your truth. Father, please bring him emotional and spiritual healing. In Jesus' name, I pray any attachments causing distress would be broken and completely surrendered to You. I pray that he would come to You in a time of need and not let pride or denial get in the way of his need for Your healing. Father, I pray You would protect our marriage from any hurts of the past and give us grace for one another if unresolved wounds arise. Help us both take healing seriously and be patient with one another. I pray we will conquer trials together with wisdom and as a team.

IN JESUS NAME I PRAY.

HEART OF GRATITUDE

*In everything give thanks: for this is the will
of God in Christ Jesus concerning you.*
1 Thessalonians 5:18

DEAR HEAVENLY FATHER,

Thank You for hearing my prayers and giving me hope for a future. I give You the praise and honor for Your everlasting love for me. I pray for my future husband's heart that he would be grateful. May he always count his blessings and not his lacks. I pray that he would stand out from the world and be different because of his mindset and attitude. I pray he would see the cup half-full instead of half-empty. I pray he will be content in whatever situation he is in and will have a thankful heart. I pray that You would remove any discontent from his heart and give him inner fullness. Lord, please help him to be a husband who walks in gratitude and appreciates me as his wife. I pray we will honor each other's efforts and be thankful for one another. I pray we will acknowledge the little things we do for each other and not take them for granted. I pray that because of his thankful heart, he will attract many more blessings into his life. May he be an example for others and use the resources You gave him to bless those in need. I pray he would demonstrate appreciation for You every day and give You glory because You are worthy of it all.

IN JESUS NAME I PRAY.

COURAGEOUS

Be strong and courageous. Do not fear or be afraid of them, for it is the Lord your God who goes with you. He will not leave you or forsake you.

Deuteronomy 31:6

DEAR HEAVENLY FATHER,

Thank You for my future husband. Please give him the confidence and the boldness to be the courageous man You created him to be. Take away any fear of men that could hinder him from standing up for what is right and being set apart from the world. I pray that he would know that he is a son of God and live from that identity. Father, please remind him that You have not given him a spirit of fear but of power, love, and a sound mind. Make him brave and strong so that he can be an example to the younger men around him and a leader in our home. I pray he would not fear men or the opinions of others but would be grounded in his faith and do what is right in Your eyes. Remind him that You are always with him and that You are for him and not against him. Remind him that You will never leave or abandon him so that he could stand confident in You. I pray he would be a man of self-control and seek refuge in You in times of weakness or doubt. In a world where godly values are trampled, I pray my future husband would have the courage to stand firm in Your truth, even if that means standing alone. Please give him the courage and a shield of faith to be able to quench all the fiery darts of the wicked.

IN JESUS NAME I PRAY.

JOY OF THE LORD

You make known to me the path of life. In Your presence, there is fullness of joy, at Your right hand are pleasures forevermore.
Psalm 16:11

Thank You, Lord, for creating my spouse more than a conqueror in Christ Jesus and an over-comer in this world. I pray for my future husband's heart and that it will be full of the joy of the Lord. I pray the joy You give him will be contagious so that people around him will catch it. May he be like a city on a hill, shining Your light to everyone around, giving You the praise. Please anoint him with Your Holy Spirit and mature his faith. I pray he will know how much he is loved and how valuable he is. Mold him into the man You designed him to be and transform him into Your likeness. Bless him with a clear mind and respectable actions. I pray he would serve You joyfully. Father, I ask You would lift any burden or distress he may be carrying because Your yoke is easy, and Your burden is light. I pray he would dwell in Your presence so much that he would experience joy even in the midst of difficulty. Teach him that joy is found in Your presence. I pray the joy of the Lord will help him navigate through life's highs and lows. I pray he would lead me as You have called him to and fulfill the role of a husband how You desire. I pray he would take refuge in You and rejoice. I pray that his heart will be full of songs and he will have a cheerful presence.

IN JESUS NAME I PRAY.

KINGDOM MINDED

Set your mind on things above, not on things of the earth.

Colossians 3:2

DEAR HEAVENLY FATHER,

Thank You for hearing my prayers. Thank You that Your ways and thoughts are higher than mine. Father, I pray for the mind of my future husband. May his mentality be kingdom-minded, and his will, be submitted to Yours. I pray You would give him a heart to passionately pursue You for the rest of his life. I pray he would desire to follow You and fulfill Your will on this earth. I pray You would seal his mind with the blood of Jesus and give him a shield of faith to protect him from any darts of the enemy. May Your Word be a lamp to his feet and a light to his path. Father, I pray You would give him a heart to always seek first Your kingdom and Your righteousness because then everything else will be added. I pray he would utilize the gifts and talents You've blessed him with for Your glory. May his desires be aligned with Your kingdom. Let him not be conformed to the ways of this world, but may he be transformed by the renewing of his mind. I pray You would give him discernment to know what is the will of God and a passion to willingly serve You all the days of his life. I pray he would prioritize pleasing and obeying You above all else. May he be completely submitted to Your will and the mind of Christ.

IN JESUS NAME I PRAY.

40

FRUIT OF THE SPIRIT

But the fruit of the Spirit is love, joy, peace, patience, kindness, goodness, faithfulness, gentleness, and self-control; against such things, there is no law.

Galatians 5:22-23

DEAR HEAVENLY FATHER,

Thank You for blessing Your body with the Holy Spirit and enabling us to bear fruit. I pray that You will touch my future husband in a special way. Please fill him with the fruit of the Spirit. Please help him to live a life by the Spirit and not the flesh. I pray he would love me like Christ loved the church and would be full of compassion and care toward those around him. I pray You would fill him with the joy of the Lord in such a way that it would be contagious. May he be a peacemaker, bringing calm to any storm around him. May he reject any strife in our marriage and avoid bitterness so that we would live in oneness. I pray he will be patient with me, listen quietly, speak thoughtfully, and choose his words wisely. I pray he would have a kind heart towards me and be mindful of how he speaks of our marriage to others. I pray that goodness would be the condition of his heart and that he would be above reproach. I pray he would be faithful with me and how he serves You. I pray he would be full of gentleness and aggression would be far from his heart. I pray my future husband will maintain self-control in his expressions and actions, especially in difficult situations. I pray the fruit of the Spirit would be evident in our marriage for Your glory and honor.

IN JESUS NAME I PRAY.

HEART OF LOVE

Love is patient and kind. Love is not jealous, boastful, proud, or rude. It does not demand its own way. It is not irritable, and it keeps no record of being wronged. It does not rejoice about injustice but rejoices whenever the truth wins out. Love never gives up, never loses faith, is always hopeful, and endures through every circumstance. Love never fails.
1 Corinthians 13:4-8

DEAR HEAVENLY FATHER,

Thank You for Your Son Jesus and for showing me the example of true love. Thank You for loving me when I was unloveable. Thank You for loving me long before I loved You. Father, I pray for my future husband's heart and ask that You would fill it with Your love. I pray Your love for him would transform him, and I pray You would show him the depths of true love and that he would love me like Christ loved the church, laying down His life for it. I pray he will be a selfless man, put others before himself, and love people the way Jesus did. I pray that he will remind me he loves me every day and show it with his actions. I pray his love for me will be unconditional. I pray that together we will be able to overcome any storms of life because we'll choose the way of love. I pray that our love for one another will grow and mature every day, so our children will have an example of what love looks like. Father, I give You his heart to keep and protect, and I trust that with You, it is safe. Thank You for creating our hearts for each other. Thank You that one day our hearts will come together, but until then, I ask that You would also prepare my heart for him and teach us sacrificial love.

IN JESUS NAME I PRAY.

DEVELOPING CHARACTER

We can rejoice, too, when we run into problems and trials, for we know that they help us develop endurance. And endurance develops strength of character, and character strengthens our confident hope of salvation.
Romans 5:3-4

DEAR HEAVENLY FATHER,

Thank You for forming my future husband in his mother's womb the way You did. I pray his character would be a reflection of Your character and heart. I pray that he would want to work on his character and model it after Christ. I pray he will always have the desire to grow and evolve and not stay the same. Help him to be more and more pleasing to You every day. Show him revelations in Your Word so he may be a leader in our home, how You intended it to be. Put Your Spirit within him and inspire him to carry out Your commands obediently. I pray he will be able to communicate respectfully and calmly with others. May he show humility and never lack fervor for doing what is right in Your eyes. Bless him, Lord, with a wise character that seeks out personal development so his light would shine brightly and people would see his good deeds and give You the glory. May he have wisdom in how to acquire a balanced lifestyle. I pray he would be thankful and satisfied with what you've blessed him with and not compare himself to others. Please give him a Christlike character that would speak with me patiently and lovingly and be sincere to those around him.

IN JESUS NAME I PRAY.

INTEGRITY

And whatever you do, do it heartily, as to the Lord and not to men. Knowing that from the Lord you will receive the reward of the inheritance; for you serve the Lord Christ.
Colossians 3:23-24

DEAR HEAVENLY FATHER,

I pray my future husband would examine his heart when needed and walk in integrity before You and the people around him. I pray he would strive to live a life mirroring how Christ walked and uphold the Biblical measure of truth. Father, please help him as a man to stand firm on the foundation of Your truth and walk tall in virtue. I pray he would be set apart from this world, challenging the status quo. I pray he would honor Your Holy Word and uphold the morals it teaches. Father, please till the soil of his heart so the fruits of the Spirit would flourish. I pray Your commandments would be written in his heart so that obeying You would come at ease. I pray he would do what is right even when no one is looking and do it heartily as if it were for You. I pray You would shape him into the husband You formed him to be. I pray that we will share similar core values so that we may be unified in our beliefs. I pray that together we will grow in truth and integrity. May we both inspire one another to live a more righteous and noble life. I pray we will be honest and sincere in our relationship and for us to trust each other effortlessly.

IN JESUS NAME I PRAY.

COMMUNICATION

Pleasant words are like a honeycomb,
sweetness to the soul and health to the bones.
Proverbs 16:24

DEAR HEAVENLY FATHER,

I ask You to bless the communication in my future marriage. May our speech with one another be full of grace, patience, and love. I pray my future husband will speak to me gently and hear me out with understanding. I pray that even if one of us really disagrees, we'd still be willing to listen and esteem each other's cares with compassion and be selfless. Please give us wisdom and knowledge so we may respect and honor one another. I pray he would be comfortable sharing his emotions with me and would not hold back in expressing himself, even in vulnerable moments. I pray that we will hear each other out and value one another's opinions, feelings, and emotions. I pray we wouldn't hold things back from each other, so nothing would build up, but rather be honest and open about everything. I pray we will truly become one, taking on each other's hurdles with serving hearts and celebrating each other's wins. I pray our marriage would be his first priority after You, Lord and that our marriage would be an unbreakable bond. Father, please bless our home to be a safe place, and may there be trust in our marriage. I pray he would be sensitive toward me and would have empathy when he speaks to me.

IN JESUS NAME I PRAY.

PHYSICAL HEALTH

Beloved, I pray that you may prosper in all things and be in health just as your soul prospers.

3 John 1:2

DEAR HEAVENLY FATHER,

Thank You for giving my future husband life. Thank You for creating him in Your image and creating him to be healthy. Father, I thank You that You are our Great Physician, and I ask that You would seal him with the blood of Jesus for protection against any illness or disease. Your Word tells us that if we drink anything deadly, it will not harm us, so I pray this promise would shield him. Father, I pray that he would keep Your commandments in his heart because Your Word tells us this will prolong life for many years, bring prosperity and bring health to the body and nourishment to the bones. I pray that he would know that healing is his for the taking, and I pray You would grant him the wisdom to know when to pick up his mat and walk in faith of his healing. I pray he would know that his body is a temple of the Holy Spirit and that he is not his own but bought with a price. I pray that he would honor You in his body and uphold a healthy lifestyle prioritizing exercise and eating healthy. I pray he would utilize the resources he has to educate himself about diet and things he could do or avoid to prevent sickness. I speak life and good health over him and ask You, Lord, to keep him safe and well all of his days.

IN JESUS NAME I PRAY.

MENTAL HEALTH

Finally, brethren, whatever things are true, whatever things are noble, whatever things are just, whatever things are pure, whatever things are lovely, whatever things are of good report, if there is any virtue and if there is anything praiseworthy—think on these things.

Philippians 4:8

DEAR HEAVENLY FATHER,

Thank You for creating my future husband to live a life of inward peace. I pray You would protect him from any dysfunctional thought patterns and bless him with a sound mind. I pray You would remove any captivity to feelings of anxiety, fear, depression, anger, confusion, or sadness. Help him to let go of things holding him back and surrender them to You. May his inner self be full of love, peace, and security in any situation. I pray for his mind to function with order and control. Please help him to be able to collect his thoughts with ease. I pray that You would sustain him and lift him up in times of need, and may he rest in peace that surpasses all understanding. Please renew his spirit daily so he will not lose focus on You. Please give him a joyful heart which is like medicine to the soul, and I pray good news will always follow him, refreshing his bones. I pray he would surround himself with company that speaks gracious words, which is like a honeycomb, sweetness to the soul and health to the body. Please remove any distractions in his life that cause him discontentment and chaos. May Your Word be his solid foundation, the yes and amen of his heart, and may he find his security in You alone.

IN JESUS NAME I PRAY.

HEARING GOD'S VOICE

*My sheep hear My voice, and I know them,
and they follow Me.*

John 10:27

DEAR HEAVENLY FATHER,

Thank You for hearing my prayers. I pray for my future husband and his ability to hear Your voice. I pray that he would be still and know that You are God. I pray he would have a strong desire to know Your will and seek counsel and guidance from the Holy Spirit. May he have ears to hear and would not only hear Your words but also put them into practice. I pray my future husband will be a man of obedience, not considering the wisdom of the world but only Your truth. I pray he would meditate on Your Word so he would be able to identify Your voice. Holy Spirit, I ask that You would remind him of the Scriptures he needs in specific moments and situations. I pray he would let You inside his heart and be vulnerable with You. I pray Your peace would cover him like a blanket and that he would bring Your presence everywhere he goes. I pray he would trust You with his life and put his confidence in You. Please help him to have faith so that when he leads our marriage, he will lead without doubt or uncertainty. Remind him of how valuable he is and that You have a purpose for his life. Give him hope for a future and show him the plans You have for him. I pray he would hold on to Your promises and recognize Your small still voice from thousands.

IN JESUS NAME I PRAY.

DISCERNMENT

Do not be conformed to this world, but be transformed by the renewal of your mind, that by testing you may discern what is the will of God, what is good and acceptable and perfect.

Romans 12:2

DEAR HEAVENLY FATHER,

Thank You for Your clarity and truth. Thank you that You're not the Author of confusion but of peace. I pray my future husband will have a strong discerning spirit so that he could choose the appropriate decisions and path to take in his life and ours. I pray his discernment would guide us on the road You want us to take and remain in Your perfect will. Please give him the willpower and strength he needs to carry out the calling You have on his life. May he walk in boldness with confidence toward the vision You gave him. I pray for the cancelation of any lies or confusion of the enemy. May he have a clear hearing of Your truth and voice. I pray You would give him discernment to know the hidden mysteries so he could be a better man in our home, leading with a clear vision of what is ahead. I pray he would be obedient to Your voice and not hinder it. Teach him to know the times we are living in and to be on guard in all seasons of life. Give him a comprehension that could only come from You. Please guard his heart and mind against becoming discouraged and disheartened. Give him faith to trust You fully, and may Your Word be his rock and solid foundation.

IN JESUS NAME I PRAY.

IDENTITY IN CHRIST

The Spirit Himself bears witness with our spirit that we are children of God, and if children, then heirs—heirs of God and joint heirs with Christ, if indeed we suffer with Him, that we may also be glorified together.
Romans 8:17

DEAR HEAVENLY FATHER,

Thank You for creating my future husband in Your image and for creating him for such a time as this. I pray he would know his true value and the price that was paid for him. I pray for his self-esteem and for You to give him confidence in who he is in Christ Jesus. May he know that he is a child of God, and I pray that You would reveal to him how You see him. Please protect his mind from thoughts that aren't from You and from intrusive thoughts. I pray he would find his identity in You, not the world's standard of recognition. I pray that You would show him the depth of Your love for him. May he find his security in You alone. I pray that his heart will feel confident and secure in the man you have called him to be. I pray he wouldn't feel pressure to live up to the world's expectations but help him remain constant in You. I pray that Your Word would saturate his heart and that You would reveal his worth to him. May he know that he is defined by who he is in Christ. I pray in our marriage, we would always uplift and remind each other that we are heirs of God and co-heirs with Jesus and live from that place.

IN JESUS NAME I PRAY.

A PURE HEART

Blessed are the pure in heart for they shall see God.

Matthew 5:8

DEAR HEAVENLY FATHER,

Thank You for hearing my prayers. I pray for my future husband and the condition of his heart. I pray he will have a pure heart and make pure choices. I pray You would give him wisdom and an awareness of his surroundings to always be mindful and responsible. May he be wise with the crowd he spends time with and set personal boundaries. I pray he would flee from temptation as Joseph did from Potiphar's wife. Father, I pray You would help him in any areas he may be struggling in, so he may live purely. May he protect our future marriage by being mindful of his actions. I pray You would surround him with Godly men who would demonstrate a pure walk. May his fleshly desires not overpower his hunger for righteousness. Remove any distractions in his life which could cause him to stumble. I pray You would give him the strength to resist sin and pursue purity. May his mind and thoughts be pure. I pray You would give him a love and desire for holiness. I pray he would take every thought captive to the obedience of Christ. May he have the desire to remain sexually pure and would honor his own body that way. May all chains of sin and bondage be broken. I pray he would protect his eyes from pornography and turn to You for strength in times of weakness.

IN JESUS NAME I PRAY.
84

WISDOM

If any of you lacks wisdom, let him ask God, who gives generously to all without reproach, and it will be given him.

James 1:5

DEAR HEAVENLY FATHER,

I pray for my future husband and ask that You would give him a mind and a heart of wisdom. I pray You would give him the fear of the Lord because that is the beginning of wisdom. I pray he would acknowledge You in all of his ways and that You would direct his path. May he counsel with the Holy Spirit in all his decisions that no man or worldly thinking would deceive or catch him off guard. I pray You would prepare the soil of his heart to take heed of Godly advice and that pride would not get in the way of growing. Give him the wisdom to lead our future conversations in a way that's full of love, compassion, and understanding. Remove any roots of pride which could prevent him from walking humbly before You and in our marriage. May the Holy Spirit teach him all things and give him the ears to hear when You speak. I pray You would give us wisdom in our marriage, to always keep You in the center and yield to Your voice and teaching. Father, as a man in our home, please give him the wisdom to test his ideas against the truth of Your Word, and I pray You would grant him a gentle Spirit of Christ so that he strives to live a worthy life for You.

IN JESUS NAME I PRAY.

HIS FAMILY

Honor your father and your mother, that your days may be long upon the land which the Lord your God is giving you.

Exodus 20:12

DEAR HEAVENLY FATHER,

Thank You for my future husband's family. I pray You would bless their lives and protect them from harm. I pray the relationship with his family is healthy and honorable. Please give them the grace to forgive, the strength to overcome any difficulties they may face, and keep them together when the world tries to pull them apart. Help them in all of their doings and draw them closer to You. I pray that he grew up with an example of a good father who taught him how to be a good husband and father. If he doesn't have a family, I pray that You would be his Father and surround him with friends who are like a family to him. Help them to live in unity and peace because You are the only one Who knows what they are going through and what weighs on them. I pray they would welcome me into their family and that there would be harmony. I pray that You would reveal Yourself to them and bring them to salvation if they are not already saved. I pray for the cancellation of any division among them if there be any. Keep them unified with love and understanding toward each other. May good health and long life prevail in their household. Comfort anyone of them fighting a silent battle, and may they find peace in You.

IN JESUS NAME I PRAY.

A GOOD FATHER

Train up a child in the way he should go, and
when he is old, he will not depart from it.
Proverbs 22:6

DEAR HEAVENLY FATHER,

Thank You for hearing my prayers, and thank You for my future husband. I pray for him and ask that You would give him a heart of a good Father. I pray my future husband is a man who seeks to be like Jesus every day and will be an example for our future children if You bless us with kids. I pray that growing up, he would have had a good father who represented fatherhood. May his lifestyle be influential and meek. Reveal to him the importance of demonstrating Christlikeness and being a good role model. I pray he will be a provider for his family and an excellent father. I pray You would create in him a humble heart willing to learn how to be a better father. Thank You, Lord, for creating my spouse in Your image and likeness. May he take on Your image in the way he interacts. Guard his mouth against speaking anything other than what glorifies You and edifies the hearer. I pray he wouldn't hold back his love but would love generously and unconditionally. May he be a beacon of light to our family. I pray he would communicate with gentleness and with love in his tone of voice. May he have fruitful habits which would make our marriage flow in balance. Please anoint his speech so his words will be uplifting and encouraging.

IN JESUS NAME I PRAY.

OBEDIENCE TO GOD

But this command I gave them: 'Obey My voice, and I will be your God, and you shall be My people. And walk in all the way that I command you, that it may be well with you.'
Jeremiah 7:23

I pray for my future husband that he would be obedient to You in all things and that You would give him the grace to listen to You always. Please help him to be obedient without compromises, and may his eye be single so his whole body would be full of light. Please protect him from darkness and give him a refined heart to walk in submission to Your will. May he see Your true goodness and be eager to follow your instructions. I pray he wouldn't grow weary in well-doing but would know that in due time he would reap a reward if he doesn't give up. I pray he would put his whole trust in You, Lord, and know that You are always just and true. Father, please guide him on the straight path and restore him to the right way if he errs. I pray his obedience to You would serve as an example to the people around him and his family. Give him the understanding that obeying You, Father, is for his very own benefit because You're a good God. I pray he would delight in Your law and Your ways. I pray he would walk before an audience of One and not be a respecter of men when it comes to doing what's honorable and obeying You. Please give him a meek heart to not be right in his own eyes but humble and accepting, ready to listen to You and good counsel around him.

IN JESUS NAME I PRAY.

MANLINESS

*For You formed my inward parts; You knitted
me together in my mother's womb. I praise
you, for I am fearfully and wonderfully made.
Wonderful are Your works; my soul knows it
very well.*

Psalm 139:13-14

DEAR HEAVENLY FATHER,

Thank You so much for creating and preparing my future husband. In the days we're living, I pray You would protect him from any attacks on his manliness, and I pray You would seal him with the blood of Jesus. May he understand his true worth and that his purpose can only be found in You. Reveal Your path for his life to him and show him the meaning of it so he doesn't wander without direction. Help him to look up to You and know that You are the Author and Finisher of his faith. I thank You for designing him to be strong so he could protect and shield our marriage. I pray for the cancelation of any confusion over his identity and for complete clarity of who You created him to be. Father, may he measure his masculinity by the way You see him and not by the standards of the world. I pray he will know that he is loved and needed and that his strengths are a blessing from You. I pray You would reveal his purpose and inspire him to look towards the future. May he cast all his worries on You, Lord. Please build him up in the knowledge of Your power and Word. Give him the gift of discernment so he may be able to understand the times and seasons.

IN JESUS NAME I PRAY.

DECISIVE LEADERSHIP

Nor as being lords over those entrusted to you, but being examples to the flock.
1 Peter 5:3

I pray You would create my future husband to be a leader in our home. I pray You would give him the wisdom he needs to lead our marriage and the discernment to make the right decisions. Please guide him on the right path so he can guide our marriage in the right direction. I pray he would be obedient to Your ways and lead us in a way that honors You and would bring a blessing to our marriage. Please give him the wisdom to resolve difficult matters which need to be addressed. I pray that You would raise him up in the midst of other godly leaders who walk in the ways of Your Word so that he would have accountability and influence of righteousness. Father, I pray You would form him into a role model for other men to walk in holiness. I pray that he will be a peacemaker leader and bring consolation to those around him. Please give him the desire to be educated in the ways of life and pursue knowledge. I pray You would give him a servant's heart with humility and equip him to lead our marriage with strength and confidence. I pray the love of Jesus will shine out of his life. May he be wise as a serpent in the middle of this corrupt generation but still harmless as a dove.

IN JESUS NAME I PRAY.

FAITHFULNESS

*One who is faithful in a very little is also
faithful in much, and one who is dishonest in
a very little is also dishonest in much.*

Luke 16:10

DEAR HEAVENLY FATHER,

Thank You for hearing my prayers. I pray for my future husband that he will be found faithful in Your eyes. I pray he would be devoted to You all the days of his life and faithful in our marriage. May he be trustworthy in the little things of life so that You may entrust him with greater things. I pray You would protect him from taking the enemy's path and protect him from the enemy's lies that lead to sin. Father, I pray my future husband will be a man of honesty and decency, so his actions will be dependable. I pray he will be a man who follows through on his promises and will be a man of his word. I pray he will be a man who walks in spiritual maturity. Father, I bring our future marriage before You and ask that You would eliminate any urges which could result in impurity, adultery, or a violated trust. Holy Spirit, please be his guide, comfort, and teach him all things, bringing to remembrance the Word in times of need. I pray that our marriage will be built on trust and that we will be faithful to one another all the days of our lives. Please remove habits that could hurt our marriage in any way. May he be pure in thought and deed and live a holy and blameless life.

IN JESUS NAME I PRAY.

GOOD COMPANY

As iron sharpens iron, so a man sharpens the countenance of his friend.
Proverbs 27:17

DEAR HEAVENLY FATHER,

I pray for protection over my future husband's circle of friends and the company he keeps. I pray You would give him the wisdom to discern which type of people are edifying to his walk with You. Father, I pray You would provide the right people in his life who would guide and lead him in ways that bring honor to You. I pray he would have a trusted accountability friend who would teach him by example to live a life that pleases You. I pray he is honored and an example to others because he lives a virtuous life. I pray he is slow to become angry and has a stillness about him. I pray his friend group would be intellectual and morally grounded. May he not compromise godly standards to entertain relationships that need to be cut off. I pray You would give him the wisdom to walk away from friendships that aren't fruitful. I pray righteous men would influence him to walk in Your ways. May his heart be humble and accept wise advice. I pray the fruits of the Spirit would be evident in his lifestyle and choice of his inner circle. Father, please bless our marriage with a good group of friends and a godly community where we would have fellowship with other believers. I pray You would provide a source of godly counsel for guidance in our marriage.

IN JESUS NAME I PRAY.

OVERCOMING SIN

Casting down arguments and every high thing that exalts itself against the knowledge of God, bringing every thought into captivity to the obedience of Christ.
2 Corinthians 10:5

DEAR HEAVENLY FATHER,

Thank You for hearing my prayers. I pray my future husband will have the strength and willpower to overcome sin. Please give him a love for holiness and a strong desire to please You every day. I pray his lifestyle would bring You honor and his life choices would be on the path of righteousness. Help him to resist the enemy so he would flee from him. I pray You would give him the wisdom to look out for things that could lead him down the wrong path and into sin. Please give him discernment and the mind of Christ, so he would allow the truth of Your Word to guide his decisions. I pray he listens to Your voice and that in time of need, You would provide a way for him to escape temptation. I pray You would give him a heart of repentance and convict him frequently and early. I pray he would have the confidence to own up to any wrongdoing. Give him a heart willing to run back to You and put his whole trust in You. Father, I ask that You would heal any wounds he may have from past sins and that You would cover him with the blood of Jesus. Thank You for Your faithfulness, Lord, and thank You for Your mercy.

IN JESUS NAME I PRAY.

PROVISION IN FINANCES

Honor the Lord with your wealth and with the first fruits of all your produce. Then your barns will be filled with plenty, and your vats will be bursting with wine.

Proverbs 3:9-10

DEAR HEAVENLY FATHER,

Thank You for hearing my prayers. I pray for my future husband that he would be ambitious and a hard worker. I pray he would stand out amongst his peers because he would work like unto the Lord, as Your Word says. I pray that as a man, he would feel satisfied and fulfilled in the type of work he does, so he is inspired to keep going. Father, I ask that You would bless the work of his hands so he would see success from his hard work. I pray he wouldn't forget to give You all the glory and, even when things are going great, to return and give You praise. Lord, please give him wisdom in knowing how to balance out work and our marriage. I ask that my future husband would be a generous man and would bless those surrounding him. I pray he would live his life out of the mindset of full abundance because Your Word says we are blessed with all spiritual blessings in heavenly places in Christ. I pray that he will be reminded daily that His blessings are a gift from You. I pray You would protect him from arrogance and that pride would not be in his heart. Instead, I pray You would give him a meek and gentle spirit and that he would work honestly. I pray he wouldn't grow weary in doing good but would know in due time he will reap a harvest if he doesn't give up.

IN JESUS NAME I PRAY.

BECOMING ONE

For this reason, a man shall leave his father and mother and be joined to his wife, and the two shall become one flesh.

Ephesians 5:31

DEAR HEAVENLY FATHER,

Thank You for the gift of life and love. I ask You to bless our future marriage and our oneness. I pray we will be compatible and complete each other. Please bless us with a harmonious and beautiful marriage that pleases You and is an example to others. Help us to die to ourselves so we can become one together. Help us to surrender our will to Your will so we can keep our marriage in peace. I pray our love for each other will grow stronger daily, and we will demonstrate it to each other. I pray we will utilize the gift of intimacy to strengthen our relationship as You created it to be. I pray for the complete restoration of any wounds and unresolved trauma. Please remove all the burdens and past brokenness that could hinder our unity together. I pray for agreement in our marriage so that we would overcome any challenges or obstacles together. I pray no hindrance would be too great that it would tear us apart. I pray we will always be best friends and enjoy each other's company. May You be glorified in our marriage, and may it be pleasing to You.

IN JESUS NAME I PRAY.

A Letter to my Future Husband

Use the blank lines to write a letter to your future husband.
One day, God willing, you could share this letter with him.

_____
Date

Delight yourself also in the Lord, and He shall give you the desires of your heart.

PSALM 37:4

PERFECT TIMING

For the vision is yet for an appointed time, but at the end, it will speak, and it will not lie. Though it tarries, wait for it because it will surely come, it will not tarry.
Habakkuk 2:3

DEAR HEAVENLY FATHER,

Thank You for your perfect timing in everything in my life, including whom I'm going to marry and when. I thank You that You're never early and You're never late. I thank You for always being on time regardless of the world's standard of timing. I thank You for always coming through for me in every other matter, and I know You will do the same in my future marriage. Father, please give me the patience I need to await the day we will meet. I trust Your perfect will, and I trust You gave me these desires for marriage, and they are not of myself. You count the number of hairs on my head, and You know all of my days. You hold the stars in the heavens and nourish the pigeons in the sky. Nothing is impossible for You, and I trust You with my future. Help me to be found faithful in this waiting period and lead my life into Your perfect will.

IN JESUS NAME I PRAY.

Personal Prayers

Until now, you have asked nothing in My name. Ask, and you will receive, that your joy may be full.

John 16:24

Use the blank lines to write down your personal prayers and desires of your heart. Our Father in Heaven is a loving Father and hears your prayers.

*But those who **wait on the Lord** shall renew their strength. They shall mount up with wings like eagles, they shall run and not be weary, they shall walk and not faint.*

ISAIAH 40:31

Share Your Thoughts

We hope this book has moved you and increased your faith. May this be the beginning of your journey in bringing your needs before our loving Father in Heaven, Who hears us.

Please take a few minutes to **write a positive review** about this book and how it has impacted your life.

- *What stood out to you?*
- *Which improvements would you suggest?*
- *Share your testimony to boost someone's faith!*

By leaving your feedback, you will help *Psalmful* create better books and journals in the future, and you will encourage someone new to discover it.

Also, please stay in touch by subscribing to our email list on *psalmful.com* to be notified of new releases and special offers.

Thank you ahead of time for helping us out! You are a blessing in this world, and we're so thankful for you.

Psalmful Team

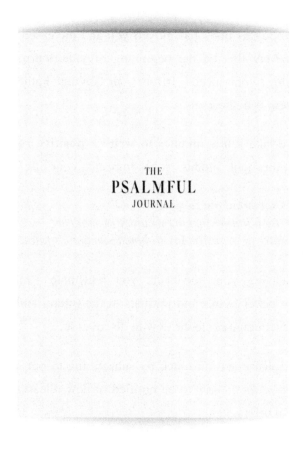

FEAUTURES:

MORNING ROUTINE

- Thanksgiving
- Prayer Requests
- Biblical Affirmations

EVENING ROUTINE

- Daily Lessons
- Counting Blessings

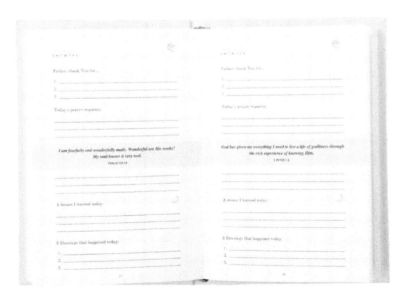

psalmful.com

Printed in Great Britain
by Amazon

27106197R00098